Original title:
A Journey Through Dreams

Copyright © 2024 Creative Arts Management OÜ
All rights reserved.

Author: Milo Harrington
ISBN HARDBACK: 978-9916-90-556-2
ISBN PAPERBACK: 978-9916-90-557-9

Shimmering Halls of Forgotten Thought

In silence whispers echo low,
Through corridors where memories flow.
Glimmers dance on fading walls,
In shimmering halls, the past enthralls.

Shadows stretch with gentle grace,
Lingering dreams in this lost space.
Fragments of laughter, whispers of tears,
In forgotten thoughts, the heart still cheers.

Frost-Kissed Dreams in Daylight's Embrace

Morning breaks with a tender glow,
Frost-kissed dreams begin to show.
The world awakens wrapped in white,
As daylight dances, pure and bright.

Each breath a cloud in shimmering air,
Fleeting visions, soft and rare.
In winter's cradle, hope ignites,
Embracing warmth in tranquil sights.

The Archway of Dusk's Embrace

Beneath the arch of fading light,
Shadows whisper, day turns night.
Colors blend in a twilight hue,
As dusk embraces the world anew.

Footsteps linger on the path unseen,
Where whispers dwell in spaces between.
The night unfolds, a mystery,
As stars awaken, wild and free.

Cosmic Cartographer's Persistence

Stars align in longing maps,
Guiding dreams through cosmic gaps.
A cartographer with pen in hand,
Charts the heart's vast, untraveled land.

Beyond the skies, where wishes soar,
In the universe's endless lore.
With patience, paths of stardust traced,
The dance of fate cannot be faced.

The Lullaby of Forgotten Dreams

In silence deep, the shadows play,
Whispers of night drift soft away.
Stars twinkle low, a gentle sigh,
While memories linger, lost in the sky.

Cradled in slumber, soft and light,
Hopes take flight in the still of night.
Winds carry tales from yesteryears,
A soothing song that calms our fears.

In every heartbeat, a story sleeps,
A lullaby that the darkness keeps.
Gentle embrace of dreams unchained,
In the quiet, all is regained.

So close your eyes, let your mind roam,
For in those dreams, you'll find your home.
In the dawn's light, they softly fade,
Yet in your heart, they'll never jade.

Celestial Migrations at Twilight

As the sun bows down to the night,
Stars awaken, a shimmering sight.
Birds of passage soar through the sky,
In twilight's embrace, they drift and fly.

Moons are rising, a silvery glow,
Guiding the lost where they must go.
Clouds weave tales of journeys untold,
In the fabric of night, their dreams unfold.

The breeze carries scents of the sea,
Whispers of places they long to be.
From twilight's hand, they find their way,
In the world of night, where shadows play.

Each star a guide, each comet a wish,
A journey of hope in the night's soft dish.
As dawn approaches, they scatter and blend,
In celestial migrations, dreams transcend.

Fables Carved in Soft Light

Once upon a time, shadows spoke,
In the glow of dusk, dreams awoke.
Stories etched in the folds of time,
Whispers of magic, a gentle rhyme.

The fire crackles, tales are spun,
Under the stars, we become one.
Each fable woven with threads of gold,
In every heartbeat, a legend unfolds.

As twilight deepens, we gather near,
Voices echo, soft and clear.
From ancient lands, to futures bright,
These fables dance in the soft light.

In every corner, a story breathes,
A tapestry rich that never leaves.
So listen closely, let your heart ignite,
In fables carved, our souls take flight.

The Refuge of Untold Sagas

In the corners of silence, stories bloom,
A refuge found in the shadows' room.
Echoes of laughter, whispers of fears,
Untold sagas born from our tears.

Time stands still in this sacred space,
Every glance tells a tale, a trace.
From ancient whispers to modern plight,
In the refuge of night, we find the light.

Each heart a book, with pages worn,
Of battles fought and love reborn.
In stillness deep, our voices blend,
A chorus of lives, we transcend.

So gather 'round, let the stories flow,
In the refuge of dreams, we come to know.
That every saga, both lost and found,
Is a thread of the tapestry all around.

Constellations of Reverie

In the night, dreams softly soar,
Whispers of stars, forever more.
Each twinkle holds a wish untold,
In the silence, magic unfolds.

Wanderers seek the cosmic light,
Guided by dreams, taking flight.
Galaxies dance in twilight's embrace,
Connecting souls in timeless space.

Through the void, thoughts intertwine,
Every heartbeat, a sacred sign.
In every glance, a universe lies,
Reflected in love's endless skies.

Together we trace the celestial stream,
Crafting our fates, realizing the dream.
In constellations, our stories blend,
An eternal journey, never to end.

Melody of the Twilit Breeze

As dusk descends with a tender sigh,
The breeze carries whispers where secrets lie.
Leaves rustle softly, a gentle refrain,
Harmonies echo as twilight remains.

Moonlight dances on the shimmering lake,
Ripples of magic the night will make.
In this moment, the world feels right,
Wrapped in the arms of the coming night.

Stars awaken, they shimmer and sing,
Tales of the heart, of love they bring.
Each note a promise, fragile yet bold,
In the melody of memories told.

With every breath, the twilight we share,
Binding our souls in the evening air.
Together we sway, in nature's embrace,
Lost in the rhythm, time holds no place.

Tides of Unseen Realities

Waves of thought crash on the shore,
Carrying truths we yearn to explore.
Beyond the surface, depths await,
In currents of fate, we navigate.

Shadows flicker in the twilight hues,
Secrets in silence, the mind's muse.
Each surge a possibility unfolds,
In whispers, the universe boldly holds.

Guided by instinct, we venture deep,
Into the dreams that we dare to keep.
In the ebb and flow of night's embrace,
We find the courage to face the space.

Time drifts like sand through open hands,
Each moment a lesson, life understands.
In this dance with unseen tides,
We grow, we learn, where wonder resides.

The Dreamscape Explorer

In realms where shadows twist and glide,
The dreamscape calls, where secrets hide.
With every step, the fabric bends,
Exploring paths where reality blends.

Figures flicker in the misty glow,
Guiding the heart where few dare to go.
Illusions dance in the moonlight's thrall,
Painting the world in colors enthrall.

Through the garden of thoughts, we wander free,
Each petal a truth, each stem a key.
Unraveling dreams, we chase the light,
In the tapestry woven of day and night.

In this journey, we find our voice,
Amidst the whispers, we make our choice.
The dreamscape opens, horizons expand,
Together we roam, hand in hand.

Threads of Imagination's Tapestry

Weaving colors of the heart,
Fingers dance on fabric's part.
Stories whispered in each thread,
Echoes of the dreams we've spread.

Patterns shift beneath the light,
Crafting visions, bold and bright.
In the loom of night, we find,
Magic spun with loving mind.

Threads connect in ways unseen,
Binding all that falls between.
With each stitch, we weave our fate,
Creating love while time awaits.

In this tapestry we weave,
Infinite tales for those who believe.
Every strand, a wish expressed,
In the journey, we are blessed.

Beneath the Gaze of Dream Weavers

Stars alight in velvet skies,
Crafting dreams where wonder lies.
With their hands, the weavers guide,
Wishes borne on night's soft tide.

Glimmers swirl in whispered streams,
Crooked paths of silver beams.
Each desire casts aglow,
Moments hidden deep below.

Echoes dance in shadowed hours,
Fragrant blooms and midnight flowers.
With every thread, a tale is spun,
Beneath the gaze, our dreams begun.

In the quiet, stillness hums,
Softest beats where magic comes.
Weavers stitching heart to soul,
Creating worlds that make us whole.

The Lanterns of Delirium

Flickering lights in the hazy night,
Casting shadows, a whimsical sight.
In delirium where dreams collide,
Lanterns glow with secrets inside.

Whispers echo in a surreal haze,
Guided by laughter, lost in a maze.
Each lantern swings with tales to spin,
Chasing the dusk as night tides begin.

Curious hearts dance in the glow,
Children of moonlight, spirits flow.
Under the lanterns, whims come alive,
In a world where imagination strives.

When dawn breaks, the magic fades,
Yet, in our hearts, the memory stays.
Lanterns of delirium, flickering bright,
Leave their glow in the fabric of night.

Reflections in Starlit Waters

Moonlit waves on a tranquil sea,
Whispering secrets, wild and free.
Stars reflected, a shimmering dance,
Holding dreams in a timeless trance.

Gentle ripples tell tales of old,
Rustic journeys in silver and gold.
With every wave, a breath we take,
In starlit waters, hearts awake.

Echoing moments, soft and sweet,
Footprints linger where waters meet.
Reflections gather, stories unfold,
In the silence, our truths are told.

Night's embrace cradles our fears,
Sailing beyond the shores of years.
In starlit waters, we shall roam,
Finding solace, forever home.

Stories Told by Flickering Shadows

In the dusk where whispers lie,
Shadows dance beneath the sky.
Tales unfold in whispered light,
Secrets bloom with falling night.

Figures wane and shapes entwine,
Echoes caught in leafy vine.
Stories born from flickering glow,
Memories of long ago.

Every glimmer tells a truth,
Fragments of enchanted youth.
In their sway, ancient echoes,
Bring to life what time bestows.

As the stars begin to gleam,
So the shadows weave a dream.
In the night, their voices blend,
A tapestry that will not end.

The Throne of Celestial Night

Upon the throne of velvet skies,
Celestial wonders fill our eyes.
Stars like jewels in deep embrace,
Guide the lost with endless grace.

Moonbeams drape the world in white,
Holding secrets of the night.
Whispers from the cosmic shore,
Call our souls to seek for more.

Galaxies spin in endless flight,
Each a tale of fiery light.
In this kingdom vast and grand,
Dreamers forge a brave new land.

Through the shadows, shadows play,
Marking time's mysterious way.
In this silence, hearts unite,
Basking in the celestial night.

Navigating Through the Dreamlit Sea

On the waves where visions glide,
Dreams embark and fears subside.
Sails of stardust catch the breeze,
Guiding hearts across the seas.

Beneath the moon's enchanting glow,
Mysteries begin to flow.
Casting nets of silver thread,
Weaving tales of those long dead.

Every ripple holds a song,
Whispers where both souls belong.
Charting courses 'midst the glow,
Navigating on the flow.

In this sea of shadows bright,
We discover hidden light.
With each tide, new paths we see,
Sailing forth through dreams set free.

Bacchanal of Imagined Streets

In the lanes where laughter rings,
Joy ignites on fleeting wings.
Imagined worlds collide and play,
Underneath the skies of gray.

Color bursts in twilight's theme,
Painting life as if a dream.
Festivals of vibrant shades,
Dance of hope that never fades.

With each corner, stories flow,
Tales of love and loss we sow.
Amidst the rhythm of the crowd,
Whispers rise and hearts feel proud.

In the bacchanal of our minds,
Every echo gently binds.
On these streets, our dreams will greet,
A celebration bittersweet.

Sailing on Clouded Waters

On dreams we drift, through mist and haze,
A boat of hope in twilight's gaze.
Guided by stars that softly gleam,
We sail the waters of a whispered dream.

The clouds below, a gentle sea,
Where every wave carries a memory.
With every breath, a chance to find,
The treasures lost within the mind.

Flickering lights in the distant night,
Illume the path, a guiding light.
Through silent whispers, past shadows cast,
We journey forth, our sails held fast.

In clouded waters, we chart our course,
With every heartbeat, a quiet force.
We write our tale on the winds of fate,
As we set sail, it is never too late.

Visions Beneath the Lunar Lake

Moonlight dances on the water's crest,
Where dreams and shadows find their rest.
Reflections whisper secrets untold,
In the depths where the night unfolds.

Stars above like diamonds gleam,
Cascading light in a silvery stream.
Beneath the surface, visions play,
Awakening hopes in the cool, soft gray.

With every ripple, stories arise,
Born of wishes, framed in sighs.
The air is thick with magic's embrace,
In this sacred, tranquil space.

As night deepens, the lake reveals,
A tapestry woven from ancient seals.
In lunar light, our spirits soar,
Beneath the sky, forever more.

When Wishes Take Flight

In the hush of dusk, dreams take wing,
Carried by whispers, soft as spring.
With every hope tucked in a sigh,
We launch our wishes into the sky.

Feathers of light in the fading sun,
Each thought a journey, no need to run.
Through open skies, they gracefully glide,
On winds of fortune, our hearts abide.

With the stars as guides, we boldly soar,
Beyond the horizon, to realms galore.
Free as the breeze, we rise above,
Chasing the echoes of dreams we love.

When wishes take flight, the world is wide,
An adventure awaits, with hearts as our guide.
In the tapestry of night, we roam,
Finding our way, forever at home.

The Map of Forgotten Fantasies

In dusty tomes of yesteryears,
Lie dreams concealed, along with fears.
Each page a treasure, a hidden clue,
Leading us back to what once was true.

Crossed lines and faded marks, a trail,
A journey embarked where dreams set sail.
With compass hearts and lanterns bright,
We seek the truths that elude the light.

Whispers of laughter, echoes of play,
In the folds of time, they never stray.
As we navigate the paths unknown,
The map unfolds, and we find our own.

In forgotten fantasies, hope survives,
With every step, our spirit thrives.
Artfully woven, the tales we weave,
In the tapestry of dreams, we believe.

Finding Home in Fading Landscapes

In shadows of the old oak tree,
Memories whisper in the breeze.
Fields once bright, now softly dim,
Nature's songs fade on the whim.

Paths we walked with eager feet,
Now lie still, a hushed retreat.
Yet in our hearts, a flame still glows,
Binding us to all we chose.

Every sunset's gentle sigh,
Calls us back to where dreams lie.
Finding home in fading lands,
Where love forever gently stands.

Through seasons lost and softly passed,
Our spirits linger, unsurpassed.
In twilight's arms, we'll find our way,
For home resides in hearts that stay.

The Ethereal Odyssey of Sleep

In twilight's veil, where dreams take flight,
The stars emerge, a soft invite.
Through realms of shadow, we begin,
An odyssey where thoughts can spin.

Soft whispers beckon, calling near,
The moonlight bathes in silver sheer.
With every breath, the world dissolves,
As secrets of the night evolves.

Through cosmic seas, we drift and sail,
On gentle waves of whispered tales.
Each lullaby, a guiding star,
In slumber's grasp, we wander far.

Within this realm, we find our peace,
In dreams' embrace, all worries cease.
Ethereal odyssey, profound,
In silent worlds, our souls unbound.

Whispers of Midnight

Beneath the cloak of midnight's breath,
The world is hushed, as shadows mesh.
Whispers travel on the cool night air,
Secrets exchanged, too light to bear.

Stars are sentinels, twinkling bright,
Guardians of our thoughts at night.
Each heartbeat syncs with cosmic rhyme,
In the stillness, we dance through time.

Moonlight spills on tranquil seas,
Guiding dreams with gentle ease.
In this hour, we find our muse,
In whispers shared, we cannot lose.

With every sigh, the night enfolds,
In silken threads, our stories told.
Whispers of midnight softly gleam,
Enveloping us in the dream.

Veils of the Somnolent Sky

The sky wraps close in evening's hue,
Veils of soft colors, deep and true.
With heavy lids, the world slows down,
As twilight weaves its velvet gown.

Stars blink softly, a tender tease,
In the calm air, we find our ease.
Each breath aligns with nature's sigh,
In the cradle of the somnolent sky.

Clouds drift lazily, shadows play,
Whispers of night gently sway.
Distant echoes of a lullaby,
Embrace the heart in quiet reply.

As dreams emerge on the horizon,
Sleep gathers close, a warm companion.
In veils of night, we find our rest,
Wrapped in peace, forever blessed.

Through the Shattered Ceiling of Night

Stars flicker like eyes, awake in the dark,
Whispers of shadows, a dance and a spark.
Beneath the vast sky, dreams scatter like dust,
Each fragment a wish, each heartbeat a trust.

The moon hangs low, a guardian bright,
Casting its glow, illuminating fright.
Through shattered glass, the night spills its charms,
Inviting the wanderer into its arms.

Clouds weave tales in silvery threads,
Of lost souls and silence, where memory treads.
Heartbeats synchronized to the universe's song,
In the still of the night, where we all belong.

Through eerie silence and echoes of light,
We traverse the cosmos, unbound by our plight.
In the whispers of stars, our stories align,
A tapestry woven, a fate intertwined.

The Celestial Pilgrim's Tale

Upon a comet's tail, I journey afar,
Tracking the essence of each distant star.
Cosmic winds sing, guiding my flight,
Through galaxies vast, a traveler of light.

I walk on the rings of Saturn's embrace,
Time bends and coils in the celestial space.
With every heartbeat, I breathe in the glow,
Of wonders unfathomed, of worlds yet to know.

Nebulas blossom in colors so rare,
Painting the void with tales rich and fair.
The wisdom of ages resides in the skies,
In silence they whisper, in starlight they rise.

A pilgrim I wander, with heart full of grace,
Embracing the darkness, for it holds its place.
In the arms of the cosmos, forever I'll roam,
A child of the heavens, the universe my home.

Secrets Beneath the Dreamer's Eye

In the depth of slumber, where shadows conceal,
Mysteries linger, unspoken, surreal.
Eyes softly closed, the world drifts away,
As the mind's canvas blooms in shades of gray.

Whispers of wishes float through the air,
Veiled in the silence, they shimmer with care.
Each heartbeat a secret, wrapped tight in a sigh,
Held close in the depth of the dreamer's eye.

Where reality falters, imagination reigns,
In this sacred realm, nothing's quite the same.
Fragments of fantasy weave through the night,
Stitching together the threads of our plight.

Awake yet ensnared in a shimmering dance,
In shadows we wander, lost in a trance.
The secrets we harbor, the dreams that we weave,
Beneath the dreamer's eye, we learn to believe.

Threads of Myth in the Dreamworld

In the fabric of dreams, where legends reside,
Threads of old myths in the night softly glide.
Stitched with the laughter of time's gentle sigh,
In the realm of imagination, the heart learns to fly.

From whispers of ancients, new stories emerge,
Like rivers of starlight, they swell and surge.
Fables entwined with the beating of hearts,
In the dreamworld they flourish, where magic imparts.

Around every corner, a creature will stare,
With tales in their eyes, and secrets to share.
The strands of our dreams interwoven with fate,
In the lore of existence, we ponder and wait.

Each night is a portal to wonders unknown,
A tapestry woven from the seeds we have sown.
In the dance of creation, forever we'll weave,
The threads of old myths, the stories we believe.

Labyrinths of Stardust Trails

In the night, we wander wide,
Through cosmic paths, our dreams collide.
With every step, the stars align,
A tapestry of fate, divine.

Whispers echo in the dark,
Guiding us with a gentle spark.
Finding solace in the light,
Lost amidst the endless night.

Each twist and turn, a hidden door,
Leading to worlds we can't ignore.
With stardust in our veins, we race,
Chasing shadows, finding grace.

The universe, a sprawling maze,
In awe, we dance through cosmic haze.
Hand in hand, we forge our way,
In labyrinths where starlight plays.

The Moonlit Quest for Lost Souls

Underneath the silver glow,
Whispers of the past do flow.
In shadows deep, the secrets lie,
As night unfolds, we seek the sky.

A journey bound by ancient lore,
We tread lightly, hearts explore.
Through haunting dreams, we find our kin,
In moonlit realms, where souls begin.

Each step reveals a tale untold,
In the stillness, the brave and bold.
With every heartbeat, we advance,
Chasing echoes, lost in trance.

Together we embrace the night,
With courage strong, we seek the light.
In shadows cast by ancient trees,
We find the peace, our hearts at ease.

Veils of Illusion

Behind the mask, the truth does hide,
In currents swift where dreams abide.
Each glimpse reveals a mirrored fate,
A fragile dance at destiny's gate.

Through painted skies, we weave our lies,
In fleeting moments, truth belies.
A tapestry of hopes and fears,
We shed the past, dissolve the tears.

In whispered tones, the night confides,
As shadows play and magic glides.
A gentle pull, the heart's allure,
In veils of illusion, we endure.

Yet in the dawn, we find our way,
Emerging from the night's ballet.
With open eyes, we face the sun,
The illusion breaks, the journey's won.

Tides of Ethereal Wonder

In waves of light, our spirits soar,
To realms unknown, we seek for more.
As tides embrace the sandy shore,
A dance of dreams forevermore.

Each crest a spark of endless grace,
We ride the currents, find our place.
With laughter high and hearts so free,
In ethereal wonder, we shall be.

Beneath the stars, the oceans sigh,
A symphony that lifts us high.
In every swell, a story swirls,
Of ancient seas and hidden worlds.

Together we'll explore the deep,
In every tide, our secrets keep.
With open hearts and dreams in tow,
We chase the wonder, let it flow.

The Enfolding Serenity of the Stars

In the night, the heavens gleam,
Luminous orbs softly dream.
Whispers of cosmos softly call,
Cradling secrets' hush enthrall.

Galaxies dance in silent grace,
Each twinkle a timeless embrace.
Infinite beauty twirls above,
Wrapped in the veil of night's love.

Moonbeams cascade, a silver tide,
Caressing the world in gentle glide.
Night's soft quilt, a tranquil sigh,
Under the vast, enduring sky.

The stars listen to wishes shared,
In this calm, hearts are bared.
Dreamers find solace in the light,
In the enfolding serenade of night.

Echoes of Ancient Sleep

In shadowed halls where memories lie,
Whispers of time float and sigh.
Dusty tomes speak stories old,
Echoing dreams that never unfold.

Beneath the surface, secrets dwell,
In every creak and shadowed swell.
The past breathes softly in the air,
Timeless tales waiting to share.

Silent echoes in the night,
Call to wanderers seeking light.
In the stillness, spirits creep,
Guiding hearts through ancient sleep.

A tapestry woven of lost refrain,
Whispers entwined with joy and pain.
In the quiet, history weaves,
A journey of souls that never leaves.

The Nurtured Heart of Whimsy

In gardens green where fairies play,
Laughter dances on the spray.
Petals twirl in playful flight,
Colors bloom in pure delight.

A breeze that teases, soft and light,
Tickles dreams that take to flight.
Sunshine spills in golden streams,
Igniting the heart of childhood dreams.

Whimsy whispers, "Join the spree,"
While time flows like a gentle sea.
With each heartbeat, joy is stirred,
In the embrace of laughter heard.

Imagination paints the skies,
With visions that enchant our eyes.
In this realm of love and cheer,
The nurtured heart finds freedom here.

Shades of Enchanted Lamplight

Underneath the willow's sigh,
Softly glows the evening sky.
Whispers dance on silver beams,
Carrying the night's sweet dreams.

Lanterns flicker, shadows play,
Guiding souls along their way.
In this realm where magic thrives,
Each heart feels the pulse of lives.

Secrets lurk in twilight's mist,
Moments held in velvet fist.
Candle flames that shimmer bright,
Illuminate the heart's delight.

Beneath the stars, together we,
Find the truth in mystery.
In the night, we lose our fears,
Dancing softly through our years.

Serpentine Road to Selah

Winding paths through ancient trees,
Carry echoes on the breeze.
Whispers call from distant pasts,
Every moment, shadow casts.

Curves that lead to hidden lands,
Where time slips softly through our hands.
In the stillness, echoes sing,
Promises the new dawn brings.

Footsteps linger, hearts entwined,
Journeys shared are never blind.
Each turn taken, stories found,
In the silence, love is crowned.

At last we pause, our breath we share,
Lost in wonder, stripped of care.
In this place, forever free,
The road unravels endlessly.

Glimmering Phantoms of the Night

Silver beams on waters clear,
Mysteries draw us ever near.
Glimmers dance on gently waves,
Where lost souls whisper through the graves.

Faintly heard, a nightingale,
Sings of dreams that still prevail.
In the moon's embrace we sway,
Chasing shadows where they lay.

Phantom forms in twilight's haze,
Guide us through a gleaming maze.
Hands held firm, we face the dark,
Light ignited by a spark.

Together, we will find our way,
In the night that holds the day.
Through the mist, our spirits soar,
Glimmering phantoms, evermore.

Serene Haven of Illusions

In a garden lost in time,
Floral scents invite to climb.
Waves of color paint the air,
Whispers of a dream laid bare.

Gentle winds caress the leaves,
Carrying tales that one believes.
Here, the heart can sit and breathe,
In the solace, we perceive.

Reflections hide in every bloom,
Filling pockets with their perfume.
In this haven, moments blend,
Crafting stories that transcend.

Illusions dance on light's sweet thread,
As we wander, hope is fed.
Serene beauty, timeless grace,
In this realm, we find our place.

Whispers of the Nocturnal Path

Beneath the silvered moon, whispers sigh,
The trees sway gently, secrets hidden nigh.
Footsteps tread softly on the soft, cool ground,
Each shadow a story, waiting to be found.

A breeze carries tales of night's sweet embrace,
While stars in their splendor, twinkle with grace.
Silken clouds drift lazily, moments unfold,
In the heart of the night, dreams beckon bold.

Night blooms with wonders, where silence sings,
In the glow of the darkness, magic takes wings.
A flicker of fireflies, dance through the gloom,
Guiding lost souls to the night's quiet room.

Awake are the whispers, a soft serenade,
The nocturnal path, where fears start to fade.
With every step taken, the soul feels alive,
In the whispers of night, our spirits arrive.

Chasing Starlit Shadows

Under the cosmic quilt, shadows entwine,
Chasing the starlight, where fates align.
Each step a heartbeat, in the still of the dark,
With dreams as our lanterns, we're set to embark.

Across the horizon, where wonders await,
In the dance of the twilight, we question our fate.
As whispers of night weave through the trees,
We follow the shadows, drifting like the breeze.

The melody of stars hums softly above,
Guiding lost hearts, leading us towards love.
Through valleys of silver, we wander with grace,
In pursuit of the shadows that time can't erase.

With every step in this celestial glow,
We're painting our stories, letting them flow.
In the chase of the night, where dreams intertwine,
We dance with the shadows, both yours and mine.

The Twilight Expedition

As daylight dwindles, the twilight calls,
An expedition unfolds as night softly falls.
With lanterns aglow, we venture ahead,
Exploring the whispers where mysteries thread.

The horizon blushes with hues of deep blue,
Guiding the lost souls to vistas anew.
Each step is a heartbeat, each pause a breath,
In the twilight's embrace, we conquer our death.

Paths crossing gently, like spirits in flight,
We gather our courage beneath the starlight.
Each shadow a promise, each whisper a guide,
On this expedition where dreams coincide.

As echoes of twilight dance in our hearts,
We move with a purpose, as magic imparts.
The journey defines us, through darkness and light,
In the twilight's embrace, we bid day goodnight.

Echoes in the Dreamscape

In the stillness of night, echoes arise,
Whispers of dreams drift beneath starry skies.
A tapestry woven of hopes and of fears,
In the dreamscape we wander, where time disappears.

With each step through shadows, the visions unfold,
Stories of wanderers, both weary and bold.
Moments frozen softly in silvery mist,
Each echo a memory, a flicker, a tryst.

The moon casts a glow on the pathways ahead,
Leading us gently where others have tread.
In the dreamscape we listen, to secrets untold,
As the night cradles whispers, both fragile and old.

With every heartbeat, we echo our truth,
In the softness of night, we reclaim our youth.
As echoes in the dreamscape serenade softly,
In the depths of our spirits, we find the key.

Portraits of the Unseen Realm

In shadows deep, their faces hide,
Whispers of dreams where secrets abide.
With every glance, a story unfolds,
Of forgotten tales and treasures untold.

A flicker, a glow, a moment caught,
In fleeting echoes, they dwell, distraught.
Their laughter lingers, a ghostly embrace,
In silent realms, they hold their place.

With colors unseen, their essence flows,
Each brushstroke paints where no one goes.
In stillness, the magic begins to weave,
Portraits of lives that we can't perceive.

Within the canvas, spirits gleam,
A dance of shadows, a cryptic dream.
They beckon softly, inviting the bold,
To step beyond what's been void and cold.

Lullabies of the Ethereal Traveler

Beneath the stars, the traveler sways,
Whispers of night in melodic arrays.
Through valleys of mist, across twilight seas,
They gather the secrets carried by breeze.

Lullabies float on the moon's silver beams,
Echoes of stories, of hopes and of dreams.
Each note a promise, a soft, tender plea,
Carried by shadows, wild and carefree.

They wander through worlds, both near and afar,
Guided by light from a distant star.
With every step, they trace ancient paths,
In lullabies woven from nature's breath.

With whispers of night, they find their retreat,
Within the embrace where the ethereal meet.
As dawn starts to break, they linger and sing,
A voyage of peace that new day will bring.

Unraveled Midsummer's Night

In midsummer's glow, where the wildflowers ignite,
Whispers of magic dance through the night.
Fireflies twinkle like stars in the dark,
As laughter and love leave their radiant mark.

Secrets are spoken beneath the soft trees,
In the arms of the breeze, a sweet, gentle tease.
The moon casts its glow on the shimmering lake,
Reflecting the dreams that we dare to awake.

Moments unravel like threads in the sky,
Imbued with the joy of a bold lullaby.
With every heartbeat, the night's stories spin,
Enchanted, we dance till the day can begin.

In this woven spell of starlit delight,
The world fades away, swallowed up by the night.
Bound by the magic, let time softly pause,
In midsummer's dream, we find our true cause.

Celestial Trails of Luminous Visions

Across the canvas of the cosmic sea,
Luminous trails spark wild, bold and free.
Whirling in rhythm, the stars weave a tale,
Of journeys profound, on a shimmering trail.

Each glimmering path, a vision to hold,
Tales of the ancients, in stardust foretold.
Through infinite depths, where galaxies twine,
Celestial whispers beckon, sublime.

With each step taken, new worlds come alive,
The pulse of the universe, fierce and contrived.
In luminous visions, we wander and roam,
Finding our place in the vastness called home.

The night unfolds secrets bathed in soft rays,
As celestial paths guide the lost through their maze.
In the heart of the cosmos, possibilities bloom,
Illuminating the dark with radiant plume.

The Path of Luminous Shadows

In twilight's hush, the whispers call,
Beneath the trees, where shadows fall.
A shimmering trail, our footsteps weave,
Guiding us on, where dreams believe.

Crickets sing in the quiet night,
Stars arise, a radiant sight.
Through tangled woods, we find our way,
The path of shadows leads to day.

Each flicker bright, a tale unfolds,
In silver light, the mystery holds.
With every step, our spirits soar,
The whispers beckon, forevermore.

In luminous glow, we dance and glide,
On this enchanted journey, we confide.
With every heartbeat, the shadows sing,
Together we roam, where hope takes wing.

Echoes of Slumbering Realms

In the silence of dreams, the echoes wait,
Gentle whispers of a world sedate.
Softly painted in shades of night,
Awakening visions, warm and bright.

Moonlit rivers flow through our minds,
Cradling secrets that fate unwinds.
A tapestry woven with threads of time,
Each moment a note, a lullaby rhyme.

Beyond the veil, where shadows linger,
Time dances slow, like a painter's finger.
The realms of slumber weave their song,
A melody sweet where we belong.

In this dreamscape, we drift and glide,
Finding solace where wonders hide.
With every heartbeat, the past entwines,
In echoes of realms, our soul defines.

Wandering Through Entity's Veil

In the silence, forms take flight,
Shadows weave in the dim twilight.
Through veils of mist, we drift and sway,
Chasing the dawn of a whispered day.

Each entity whispers a forgotten lore,
Stirring the heart with tales of yore.
Voices blend in the twilight's breath,
Guiding us gently through the face of death.

In flickers of light, we lose our ground,
A dance in the dark, where dreams are found.
Wandering softly, embracing the thrill,
Through the veil, we seek, we will.

With every step, the mystery grows,
In the depths of shadows, the whisper flows.
Connected by threads of the unseen trail,
Together we wander, through entity's veil.

Liquid Stars and Floating Thoughts

In the night sky, liquid stars gleam,
Dreams cascade like a flowing stream.
Thoughts take flight on shimmering beams,
A dance of wonder, a cosmic dream.

Floating softly like feathers in air,
Ideas drift, both gentle and rare.
In the quiet stillness, they twirl and spin,
A universe swirling deep within.

With every heartbeat, a new star shines,
Illuminating the paths of minds.
Liquid thoughts swirl in endless play,
Guiding our voyages through night and day.

Together we wander, through galaxies vast,
Finding our place in the shadow cast.
In liquid stars, our secrets unfold,
Floating thoughts shimmer, a story told.

Radiant Pathways to Unknown

In twilight's glow, we walk the lane,
Whispers of dreams call out our names.
With every step, the shadows wane,
Guiding our hearts through uncharted games.

Stars above like lanterns bright,
Illuminating routes we dare to find.
Together we chase the silver light,
Wandering where hope and courage bind.

Through tangled woods and winding streams,
The scent of wildflowers fills the air.
We dance along the edge of dreams,
Embracing the magic hidden there.

A journey awaits in each heartbeat's song,
Radiant pathways leading us on.
In the unknown, we find where we belong,
Hand in hand, we'll greet the dawn.

The Serenade of Sighs and Stars

In the quiet night, the stars ignite,
Casting their glow on hearts that yearn.
A serenade of sighs takes flight,
Longing and love in every turn.

Beneath the moon, secrets unfold,
Whispers carried on the midnight breeze.
Stories of lovers from days of old,
Entwined in a dance with such sweet ease.

Echoes of laughter blend with our dreams,
A melody rising, soft and clear.
In this moment, nothing is as it seems,
For in the dark, we shed our fear.

As constellations shimmer above,
Our hearts entwined in celestial ties.
The serenade speaks of endless love,
Beneath the sighs, our souls arise.

Sculpting Realities in Slumber

In the realm where shadows play,
We carve our dreams from stardust light.
With weary hearts, we drift away,
From waking worlds we take our flight.

Each vision dances through the night,
Sculpting truths from whispers low.
In twilight's arms, time feels just right,
Unraveling dreams only we know.

Mirrors reflect what we can't speak,
In slumber's hold, our spirits rise.
Creating realms, unique and sleek,
Where silence sings and laughter flies.

Awake we wander, yet in sleep,
Reality bends, and worlds entwine.
Sculpting wonders, we dig deep,
Our dreams, our treasures, forever shine.

Beneath the Haze of Daybreak

Morning whispers through the mist,
Sunlight breaks, the shadows fade.
In this hush, dreams coexist,
Beneath the haze, our fears dismayed.

The world awakens, colors blend,
Gentle hues embrace the day.
With every breath, our spirits mend,
Rising high as night gives way.

Nature's chorus fills the air,
A symphony of life reborn.
With open hearts, we shed despair,
As dawn unveils the promise sworn.

Beneath the haze, we find our grace,
In every heartbeat, every sigh.
Together we welcome this sacred space,
Where dreams take flight and hopes can fly.

Wings of the Night Wanderer

In shadows deep, the night takes flight,
A solitary figure glides from sight.
With whispers soft, the moon does call,
She dances on dreams, enchanting all.

Across the sky, where silence reigns,
The stars align like silver chains.
With every beat, her heart ignites,
A symphony of dark delights.

The world below in slumber's hold,
Her wings unfurl, a tale unfolds.
Through twilight's realm, she roams so free,
A spirit bound, yet never we.

In night's embrace, she finds her truth,
A fleeting glimpse of vibrant youth.
With every dawn, the magic fades,
Yet still, she flies through twilight glades.

Beyond the Veil of Slumber

A dreamer lies where shadows blend,
In realms unknown, where thoughts ascend.
Beyond the veil, the secrets sigh,
As wishes float on midnight's cry.

Through velvet skies, the stars ignite,
Casting spells that dance in light.
In whispered tones, the spirits call,
Inviting hearts to leap and fall.

A tapestry of hopes and fears,
Woven tight with dreams and tears.
Each thread a story, rich and bright,
Unfolding softly through the night.

To wake anew, a whispered prayer,
As dawn unfolds with gentle care.
Yet in that space, where dreams often loom,
Lies the magic of twilight's bloom.

Serpents of the Sleeping Mind

In slumber's hold, they twist and coil,
Visions rise from a dreamer's toil.
Serpents glide through thoughts so deep,
Winding pathways where shadows creep.

With silent grace, they weave and play,
Unraveling fears, come what may.
In midnight's hush, they silently find,
The tangled truths of a sleeping mind.

In whispers soft, they stir the heart,
Unfold the tales that break apart.
From buried seeds of hopes long dashed,
They kindle flames where shadows splashed.

Awake, yet lost in tangled threads,
We chase the whispers, follow the leads.
In every plait, a story framed,
Serpents of thought, forever unnamed.

Driftwood on Cloud Rivers

On currents soft, the driftwood sways,
Floating gently through sunlit bays.
Cloud rivers beckon, lush and wide,
Where dreams reside and spirits glide.

Beneath the sky, where echoes play,
Each moment captured, night and day.
With whispered winds, they drift along,
Carried forth by nature's song.

A journey spun of time and fate,
Each piece of wood a heart, innate.
In tranquil flows, they find their place,
Cradled in the universe's embrace.

Together they weave, a tale of grace,
Of life's embrace, of love's sweet trace.
In wooden whispers, stories arise,
Driftwood dreams beneath vast skies.

Sailed on the Ship of Fancies

We set our sails to the wind's soft call,
With laughter and dreams, we dared to sprawl.
On waves of wonder, our spirits danced,
In the sea of creation, our hearts entranced.

The stars above whispered tales of old,
Each twinkle a wish, a story retold.
With every gust, new worlds we found,
In the magic of night, our hopes unbound.

The horizon beckoned, a promise so near,
We voyaged through waters of joy and fear.
Together we traveled, hand in hand,
On the ship of fancies, a dreamer's band.

As dawn painted skies with a golden hue,
We gazed back in awe, the vastness grew.
For our hearts were light, and our minds were free,
Sailed on the ship, just my dreams and me.

The Mirage of the Dream Weaver

In twilight's glow, shadows gently sway,
Weaving dreams in the dusk of day.
A tapestry spun of hopes and fears,
Translucent visions, from laughter and tears.

The dream weaver calls with a silken thread,
Each knot tied tight, a story unsaid.
In colors that shimmer, the secrets unfold,
In the heart's quiet chambers, a magic bold.

With whispers of light, the night takes shape,
New worlds bloom as the boundaries gape.
Each flicker of thought, a star in the mind,
A mirage of life, entwined and refined.

In the dreamscape where shadows gleam,
Reality slips, like sand through a seam.
Awakened by magic, I chase the surreal,
The dance of the dream weaver, so vivid, so real.

Ascent to the Etheric Heights

We climbed the stairs of the endless night,
Each step a heartbeat, a flickering light.
With courage as wings, we reached for the skies,
In the breath of the cosmos, we learned how to rise.

The ether called softly, a melodic hum,
Whispers of wisdom, a rhythm we'd strum.
As constellations painted the canvas above,
We soared through the silence, embraced by love.

In heights of existence, the soul took flight,
Dancing with shadows, weaving through light.
The echoes of dreams lingered on the breeze,
As we reached for the stars with elegant ease.

In the glow of the dawn, our spirits would blend,
An ascent to the heights, with no need to end.
Together in rapture, we spanned the great void,
In the realm of the ether, our hearts were not coy.

The Realm of Ethereal Echoes

In the realm of whispers where echoes reside,
Soft melodies linger, like waves of the tide.
Each sound a caress, a story refined,
In the canvas of silence, our souls intertwined.

Threads of the past weave through the air,
Visions of life float, fragile and rare.
Within the soft glow, memories dance light,
Cradled by shadows that linger at night.

With every heartbeat, a resonance grows,
A symphony breathing where the heart knows.
The echoes remind us of all that we've sought,
In the realm of the echoes, we find what we've fought.

Together we traverse this ethereal land,
In the whispers of time, we take each other's hand.
In the embrace of the echoes, forever we'll stay,
In the realm of the unseen, where love lights the way.

The Enchanted Drift

In whispers sweet, the breezes flow,
Through ancient trees, where secrets grow.
A glimmering path of silver light,
Guides weary souls through the deep night.

The moon above, a watchful gaze,
Illuminates the hidden ways.
With every step, the heart will soar,
In dreams awakened, forevermore.

Stars collide in a dance divine,
Painting the sky, a celestial sign.
In the enchanted drift of time,
We lose ourselves, in rhythm and rhyme.

As morning dawns, the magic fades,
Yet in our hearts, the journey stays.
For in the drift, our spirits blend,
A timeless tale that shall transcend.

Footprints on the Ether

Upon the clouds, where shadows drift,
We tread the path, a cosmic gift.
With every step, we leave a trace,
Of fleeting thoughts in endless space.

The stars above, they call our name,
In constellations, wild and tame.
With footprints light on air we share,
A journey woven with tender care.

The winds will carry whispers bold,
Of stories past and dreams retold.
In ethereal realms, we dance and play,
As night gives way to the break of day.

In twilight's hue, our spirits soar,
Each heartbeat echoes, forevermore.
For footprints on the ether remain,
A testament to joy and pain.

The Secret Garden of Night

Beneath the stars, in silence deep,
The secret garden begins to sleep.
With petals soft and fragrance rare,
Whispers linger in the evening air.

Moonlight dances on silver streams,
Awakening wild and wondrous dreams.
In hidden nooks, where shadows play,
The garden blooms in a mystical way.

Each blossom holds a sacred tale,
Of ancient hopes and whispered wail.
In the night's embrace, we find our peace,
As worries fade and troubles cease.

The secret garden, a world apart,
Nestles gently within the heart.
With every breath, we come alive,
In the tender night, where dreams can thrive.

Chasing the Twilight Mirage

In colors deep, the dusk unfolds,
A tapestry of tales retold.
The horizon blushes, soft and wide,
As day surrenders to the tide.

Chasing the mirage, we feel the lure,
Of fleeting moments, bright and pure.
With every breath, the magic swells,
In fleeting whispers, the twilight dwells.

Each shadow lengthens, a dance of grace,
As stars emerge to take their place.
With hearts aglow, we brave the night,
In search of dreams that feel so right.

As twilight fades into the night,
We hold our hopes with all our might.
For in the chase, we find our way,
In the mirage's glow, we long to stay.

The Color of Twilight's Breath

Whispers of purple kiss the sky,
As day and night softly collide.
Crimson clouds, like dreams, drift high,
In this moment, all worlds abide.

A gentle breeze stirs the calm,
Carrying scents of fading light.
Nature's peace is a soothing balm,
In twilight's embrace, hearts ignite.

Stars awaken, shy and bright,
While shadows stretch and softly play.
In hues of gray and fleeting light,
We find the magic of the day.

With each breath, dusk finds its depth,
Painting silence with grace so rare.
The night whispers secrets kept,
In twilight's glow, we breathe the air.

Lost in the Maze of Night's Heart

In the shadows where dreams entwine,
A labyrinth of echoes calls.
Silent footsteps on paths divine,
Through whispered hallways, the darkness sprawls.

Moonlight dances on jagged stone,
Guiding hearts that seek the way.
Each turn reveals the unknown,
In the night, we choose to stay.

Faces flicker in candlelight,
Lost in thoughts that drift and weave.
In the struggle between wrong and right,
We find solace in what we believe.

Yet in the maze, love's spark ignites,
A compass for weary souls.
In the dark, we'll find our sights,
Together, we become whole.

Wisdom from the Oracle of Sleep

In slumber's arms, the world retreats,
Dreams whisper tales of ancient lore.
Through time and space, our spirit meets,
In silent shadows, we explore.

The oracle speaks in hushed tones,
Guiding us through the night's embrace.
In each vision, wisdom hones,
Unfolding truths in twilight's grace.

Each dream a puzzle, softly spun,
Guiding hearts to what lies beyond.
In realms of night, we are but one,
Where thought and spirit dance and bond.

Awake we'll rise with morning light,
Yet carry wisdom deep inside.
For in the dark, we find our flight,
And through our dreams, the truth will guide.

Dreams as Tapestries Woven

Threads of gold in the twilight thread,
Colors dance in the midnight glow.
Every dream, like a whisper said,
Woven tales of joy and woe.

Stitching pieces of heart and mind,
Creating patterns of who we are.
In each knot, our hopes entwined,
Guiding us like a distant star.

With every seam, stories to tell,
Tangled paths in the fabric swirl.
In the loom of night, we dwell,
As dreams unfurl and gently twirl.

Embrace the art with open eyes,
For each thread symbolizes fate.
In every dream that softly flies,
We find ourselves, we recreate.

Threads of Moonlight Flutter

In the quiet night sky, the moon takes flight,
Silver threads dancing in gentle light.
Whispers of dreams drift like soft sighs,
Carried on breezes where beauty lies.

Stars twinkle above, a celestial choir,
Guiding the way with their soft, warm fire.
The world below paints in shadows and glow,
As moonlight flutters, weaving tales we know.

Each shimmering ray a story to tell,
Of hopes and desires, of love's sweet spell.
Nestled in darkness, the heart learns to see,
The magic of night, wild and free.

So let's dance in the glow of this silver beam,
Chasing the echoes of a half-formed dream.
For in this moment, together we soar,
Threads of moonlight flutter, forevermore.

The Secret Symphony of the Night

Beneath the velvet sky, secrets unfold,
A symphony whispers in melodies bold.
Crickets play softly, a rhythmic refrain,
As night wraps around like a gentle chain.

The cool breeze carries a delicate tune,
Dancing through trees, beneath the bright moon.
Owls serenade softly, their voices aligned,
In the echoing stillness, nature entwined.

Stars hum a chorus, a luminous band,
Playing the notes of this wondrous land.
In shadows and whispers, the magic takes flight,
Revealing the beauty locked deep in the night.

So listen closely, let your heart hear,
The secret symphony, vibrant and clear.
In the hush of the night, embrace the delight,
For every soft sound ignites the soul's light.

Whispers in the Land of Faerie

In the land of faerie, where magic prevails,
Whispers of wonders ride on the gales.
Tiny lights flicker in the soft twilight,
Guiding lost travelers with joy and delight.

Flowers bloom brightly in colors so rare,
Spreading sweet fragrances through crisp, cool air.
Laughter and song fill the glen with mirth,
Cradled like treasures deep within the earth.

Glimmers of gold fall like dew from the sky,
As faeries weave dreams with a twinkling sigh.
Here every secret is stitched with a thread,
Of laughter and love, where all fears are shed.

So wander these meadows, let your heart soar,
In the land of faerie, you'll find so much more.
For in whispered breezes, true magic we find,
Living forever in the heart and the mind.

Beneath the Cocoon of Wishes

Beneath the cocoon of wishes we dream,
A tapestry woven with each fanciful beam.
Stars stitched together in a quilt of night,
Guarding our hopes with their soft, gentle light.

Each wish is a feather, light as the air,
Floating on currents, with grace and with care.
Held close to the heart, they dance and they sway,
Carried on breezes that softly play.

With every heartbeat, a whisper takes flight,
Unlocking the realms of purest delight.
For in this cocoon, we find solace and peace,
A moment of magic, where burdens release.

So close your eyes gently and breathe in the night,
Wrap yourself warmly in ethereal light.
Beneath the cocoon of wishes we lay,
Dreaming our dreams until beckoned by day.

Portals to the Brume

In shadows deep, the mist unfolds,
Step lightly now, let fate be told.
Whispers call from veils of gray,
Through silent paths, we drift away.

Ethereal hands, they guide our way,
To lands where night turns into day.
Each footfall echoes, soft and slow,
As silver beams begin to glow.

The brume may hide, yet hearts can see,
The shimmering truth that sets us free.
Through hidden doors of dreams we roam,
In every breath, we find a home.

So step with care, and breathe it in,
For in this realm, all tales begin.
With every step, our spirits rise,
In portals lost 'neath twilight skies.

Threads of Time from the Abyss

In shadows spun, the weavers dance,
Through threads of time, they cast a glance.
Moments linger and fade like mist,
In the abyss where dreams exist.

From echoes born of silent screams,
The tapestry unravels dreams.
A timeless knot, a fateful thread,
Binds the living, the lost, the dead.

With every pull, the past ignites,
While future glimmers like distant lights.
In woven paths, our fates entwine,
Through threads unbroken, we align.

So heed the whispers in the gray,
For time, in truth, will never stay.
Embrace the ebb, the flow, the kiss,
Of threads that lead us from the abyss.

Frosted Leaves of a Silent Dream

On branches bare, the snowflakes gleam,
Frosted leaves weave a silent dream.
Beneath the sky, where whispers fly,
Nature sighs in a soft lullaby.

The world is hushed, in winter's hold,
Stories wrapped in silver and gold.
Each delicate flake, a memory spun,
In landscapes silent, all becomes one.

A moment caught, where time stands still,
In frosted realms, we feel the chill.
Yet in this cold, a warmth remains,
In every breath, our essence reigns.

So wander far, through dreams embraced,
In the stillness, find your place.
For in the frost, life's truth may gleam,
Amidst the leaves of a silent dream.

Enchanted Labyrinths of Mesmer

In realms where echoes gently play,
Labyrinths lead our thoughts astray.
With every turn, a secret spark,
In shades of light and whispers dark.

The paths we tread, both lost and found,
In enchanted circles, we are bound.
Each corner turned, a choice unfolds,
As magic weaves its tales of old.

A dance of shadows, flickers bright,
In mesmerizing twists of night.
Through winding ways, we seek our peace,
In tangled fates, our souls release.

So wander forth, embrace the maze,
In every moment, find the gaze.
For in this dance of hearts and minds,
We find the truth that life unwinds.

The Silent Voyage Within

In the depths of quiet seas,
Soul sets sail on whispered breeze.
Stars above, a guiding light,
Navigating through the night.

Thoughts like waves, they ebb and flow,
In this realm, the heart will grow.
Dreams awaken, spirits soar,
Finding treasures on the shore.

Echoes of the past align,
Woven in the fabric fine.
Every heartbeat, every sigh,
Tales of journeys that comply.

At journey's end, a mirror found,
Reflections deep, but truth profound.
In silence, wisdom's voice will call,
Embrace the voyage, rise or fall.

Glimmers of the Sleepwalker

In shadows cast by dimming light,
Dreamers dance on edges bright.
Whispers flutter, secrets shared,
In this world, the heart is bared.

Footsteps soft on twilight's edge,
Each quiet thought, a whispered pledge.
Eyes half-closed, they roam the night,
Searching for the spark of light.

Through the veil of slumber's grace,
They find warmth in a gentle space.
Glimmers twinkling in their soul,
As silent echoes start to roll.

Awake or dream, who can define?
Both realms hold a thread, entwined.
In sleep's embrace, they find their way,
Chasing shadows till the day.

Shattered Mirrors of Imagination

Reflections fracture, colors blur,
In a world where visions stir.
Breaking barriers of the mind,
New creations burst, unconfined.

Each shard tells a tale untold,
Memories wrapped in glimmers bold.
Fractured dreams conjoin and bend,
From chaos, art begins to mend.

Visions dance like fleeting smoke,
In this realm, the heart awoke.
Textures merge in vibrant hues,
Crafting worlds with every muse.

Imagination takes its flight,
Chasing shadows, seeking light.
Through shattered mirrors, clarity gleams,
A tapestry of fractured dreams.

The Horizon of Reveries

At dawn's first blush, dreams take flight,
Colors painting the canvas bright.
Horizons stretch beyond the sea,
Where echoes of hope whisper free.

In golden rays, imaginations bloom,
Casting aside the vestiges of gloom.
Waves serenade the shores of thought,
In every heart, a journey sought.

Clouds drift past, like fanciful fears,
Carried by winds that dry the tears.
Each heartbeat pulses, a rhythmic cue,
Guiding the soul to visions anew.

With every dusk, the world transforms,
In the realm of dreams, all norm reforms.
The horizon gleams with endless desire,
A tapestry woven from hope's vibrant fire.

Sunrises in the Land of Whispers

Golden hues spill across the sky,
Awakening dreams that softly sigh.
Mountains greet the light with grace,
Nature stirs in a tender embrace.

A breeze carries secrets from afar,
Guiding the dawn, a glimmering star.
Birds sing melodies of hope and cheer,
Echoing promises of another year.

The rivers dance in morning's glow,
Reflecting stories the waters know.
Fields awaken to a colorful quilt,
In the land of whispers, magic is built.

Each sunrise a canvas, a fresh new start,
Painting the world with an artist's heart.
In silence, the daybreak finds its way,
In the land of whispers, come what may.

The Celestial Driftwood

Waves roll gently on the sandy shore,
Driftwood whispers tales of yore.
Stars above like jewels so bright,
Guiding lost souls through the night.

Each piece of wood a story to tell,
Eons of time within them dwell.
Carved by the sea's relentless hand,
Silent witnesses to the land.

Under the moon's soft, silver glow,
The driftwood breathes, its essence flows.
Nature's treasures, timeless and wise,
Speak of journeys beneath the skies.

In the twilight, their shadows blend,
Drifting dreams where horizons end.
The celestial driftwood calls my name,
In its embrace, I find my flame.

Tracing Shadows in Midnight Glades

Through the thick woods where whispers hide,
Midnight glades beckon, shadowed and wide.
Moonlight dances on leaves so green,
A magical world, serene and unseen.

Footfalls soft on the forest floor,
Echoing secrets that never bore.
Creatures stir in the cool of night,
Woven in darkness, waiting for light.

Glimmers of silver break through the trees,
Carrying fragrances on a gentle breeze.
Every shadow a story to share,
In midnight glades, magic fills the air.

With each step, the past intertwines,
A tapestry rich in mystic designs.
Tracing shadows in time's embrace,
In the heart of the glade, I find my place.

The Enigma of Astral Echoes

In a realm where the stars collide,
Whispers of cosmos gently glide.
Galaxies twirl in a timeless dance,
Echoes of fate in a cosmic trance.

Nebulas cradle the dreams we weave,
Fragments of light that we believe.
Every echo a tale yet untold,
Woven in silver, threads of gold.

Constellations map the hearts we seek,
Stories of passion, whispers unique.
In the silence, the magic flows,
The enigma of astral echoes grows.

With each pulse of the endless space,
We chase the wonders, embrace the grace.
In the night sky, the answers lay,
In the enigma, we find our way.

Among the Fantasies We Dwell

In twilight's embrace, whispers collide,
Where shadows paint the dreams we hide.
A tapestry woven with threads of the night,
In the depths of our hearts, they take flight.

Through gardens of wonder and realms of delight,
We chase fleeting moments, like stars burning bright.
Each laugh a melody, each sigh a soft breeze,
Among the fantasies, we find our ease.

Dreams dance like fireflies, glowing so near,
In the cool, gentle dusk, all our hopes appear.
With every heartbeat, new visions unfold,
In the stillness of night, our stories are told.

So let us wander, hand in hand,
Through landscapes of magic, forever we stand.
For among the fantasies, love will prevail,
Together we'll flourish, together we'll sail.

Treading the Boundless Abyss

In the depths where shadows creep,
I tread the silence, secrets to keep.
The dark calls softly, luring me near,
Each breath a whisper, each pulse a fear.

Endless horizons stretch far and wide,
In the void, I wander, curious and tied.
Stars flicker dimly, like thoughts in my mind,
In this boundless abyss, solace I find.

With every step taken, new truths arise,
Unraveling layers, shedding disguise.
What once was formless, now starts to shape,
In shadows' embrace, I learn to escape.

Emerging from darkness, a spark ignites,
The power of choice in the stillest of nights.
So treading I am, in spaces less known,
Finding new strength, as I make them my own.

The Carousel of Forgotten Dreams

Round and round, the colors spin,
Memories linger, where years begin.
Each horse a story, a tale to be told,
In the carousel's heart, the young and the old.

Whispers of laughter, echoes of hope,
As time weaves a tapestry, teaching us to cope.
A waltz with the past, a dance with the now,
In the circle of dreams, we all take a bow.

Fading reflections in the twilight's grace,
Each moment we cherish, a soft, warm embrace.
From dreams long forgotten, we gather the light,
In the carousel's spin, we remember the night.

So let the music play, let the lights sway bright,
As we gather our dreams, igniting the night.
For in this carousel, all souls align,
In the mingling of wishes, forever we shine.

Navigating Wisps of Fantasy

In the ether's embrace, where fancies collide,
I chart a course where dreams softly glide.
With each gentle turn, the whispers grow bold,
As unseen worlds unfold, stories retold.

Through misty horizons, I sail with delight,
Chasing the wisps, kissed by moonlight.
The stars trace my path, guiding my way,
In the heart of the night, where night meets the day.

Emotion like currents, flowing and free,
Drifting on breezes, just you and me.
We dance in the shadows, we laugh with the dawn,
Through fantasies woven, our spirits are drawn.

So here in this realm, let our hearts be the guide,
Navigating wisps where our secrets abide.
For as we explore all the wonders that gleam,
Together we'll wander, together we'll dream.

Through the Crystal Lattice

In the shimmer of fractured glass,
Light dances, a fleeting mass.
Colors collide in a silent fight,
Each hue whispers, taking flight.

Reflections cast on the floor,
Echoes of dreams we explore.
Through prisms bright, secrets unfold,
Stories of beauty, softly told.

Beneath the surface, layers hide,
Truths and fantasies collide.
In the maze of complex design,
Nature's wonders intertwine.

Glimmers caught in time's embrace,
Moments lost in a fragile space.
Each shard tells a tale, unique,
Through the crystal, we seek the peak.

The Echo Chamber of Silent Hopes

In shadows deep where whispers bloom,
Hopes resonate within the room.
Silent yearnings find their voice,
In the heart, they seed their choice.

Each echo carries dreams alight,
Fueling courage in the night.
Visions woven through the air,
Landscapes painted, bold and rare.

Vibrations soft, yet strong they rise,
Beneath the starlit, endless skies.
In the chamber, truths combine,
With every pulse, paths intertwine.

Listen close, the echoes call,
Through the silence, we stand tall.
Each heart a vessel, hope confined,
Breaking free, our dreams aligned.

Labyrinthine Reflections of Light

In a web where shadows twine,
Reflections dance, they intertwine.
Layers thick with mystery,
Reveal the heart of history.

Winding paths of gleaming rays,
Lead our minds through endless maze.
Every turn, a story spun,
Fragments speak, the journey's begun.

Illuminate the hidden truth,
Through the laughter, through the ruth.
In this labyrinth, wisdom glows,
Guiding us where the river flows.

The flickering light, it knows our name,
In every sorrow, in every flame.
Through the twists, we seek our fate,
In reflections, hesitate, create.

Between the Veils of Night

In twilight's grace where shadows blend,
Stars emerge, like whispered friends.
The veil of night wraps tight in folds,
Secrets deep and tales untold.

Beneath the moon's soft, silver light,
Dreams awaken from the night.
Glimmers spark where silence dwells,
Enchantment lingers, magic swells.

With every sigh, the dark reveals,
Voices lost, the heart now heals.
Between the layers, courage found,
In darkness, our hopes unbound.

Rest in shadows, let time weave,
A tapestry we shall believe.
Fading dreams return to sight,
Awakening between the night.